SUCCESSFUL COOKING

EASY PASTA

INDEX

Contents

Perfect Pasta

Throw some pasta into a pot of boiling water and while it bubbles away, cook up a simple sauce and you have a deliciously easy meal.

USING THIS BOOK

There are five main shapes of pasta: short, curly, long, filled and flat. For something a little different, we have divided our recipes into chapters that reflect the shape of the pasta they use. The same pasta may go by different names around the world, so, to help you identify the pasta shapes we have used, there is a helpful mini glossary at the start of each chapter. The glossary not only helps identify the different pasta types, but also gives some possible substitutions.

STORING PASTA

Dried pasta can be stored in a cool dry place for months. Fresh pasta must be refrigerated and won't keep for very long, so buy it as you need it. Filled pasta is best bought a day or so before you need it, but some vacuum-packed filled pastas can be kept for up to 3 weeks (check the use-by date). It can be frozen in a single layer between sheets of plastic wrap for up to 3 months but creamy fillings don't freeze well.

MATCHING SAUCE TO PASTA

With up to 300 different pasta shapes, it can be confusing knowing which sauce to serve with which pasta shape. A basic rule to remember is that a chunky pasta is best with a chunky sauce and a thin pasta is best with a thin sauce. Chunky pasta shapes enable you to pick up the

sauce with the pasta. Smooth, slender pasta shapes will not hold a chunky sauce but will suit a sauce of olive oil or a fresh tomato sauce. Tiny pasta such as ditalini or stelline are usually used in soups.

HOW MUCH PASTA?

As pasta varies so much in shape, size and type, it is hard to be specific about how much pasta you need per serve. The chart below gives some basic guidelines about how much pasta to provide.

COOKING PASTA

Pasta should be cooked in a large, deep saucepan of water to allow room for expansion and to prevent it sticking together. Allow about 6 litres (24 cups) of water for every 500 g (1 lb 2 oz) pasta, but never use less than 4 litres (16 cups). Filled pasta and large pasta, such as lasagne, will need more water (9–12 litres/36–48 cups), as they are more likely to stick.

If you need to cook large amounts of pasta, cook up to 1 kg (2 lb 4 oz) of pasta per saucepan.

Always bring the water to the boil before stirring in the pasta. When the water comes back to the boil, begin timing, stirring often once the pasta softens a little. Test the pasta just prior to the final cooking time.

Adding oil to the pasta while cooking contributes very little, but seasoning the water with a little salt can add to the flavour. This is entirely a matter of personal preference.

COOKING TIME

Cooking times for pasta vary enormously depending on the size, shape and freshness of the pasta. Generally, the fresher the pasta, the shorter the cooking time. Fresh pasta from a delicatessen or pasta shop usually only needs 1–2 minutes. Vacuum-packed fresh pasta from the supermarket requires a little longer – about 6 minutes. Dried pasta varies depending on the size and shape but because it needs rehydrating as well as cooking, it usually takes longer than fresh pasta. For the most accurate times for all pasta, follow the instructions on the packet.

The best way to ensure pasta is cooked is to taste it. The pasta should be just tender, not at all raw or soft and gluggy. This is referred to in Italian as al dente which literally means 'to the tooth'.

SERVING UP

Once the pasta is cooked, it is important to drain it in a colander and then turn it either into a heated dish, the pan with the sauce or back into its cooking pan.

Don't overdrain the pasta: it needs to be a little wet for the sauce to coat it well. Never leave pasta sitting in the colander or it will clump together. A little olive oil or butter tossed through drained pasta will prevent it from sticking together.

Never rinse the pasta unless stated in the recipe: it is usually only rinsed if used in a baked meal or served cold in a salad because the starches released in cooking the pasta help it meld beautifully with the sauce.

Timing is essential when preparing a pasta meal. The sauce should be ready as soon as possible after the pasta is cooked because pasta continues to cook if left to sit around and can become soggy and unappetising.

Pasta Shapes

SHORT

THESE PASTA SHAPES REFUSE TO BE OVERLOOKED: THEIR VERSATILITY MEANS THEY CAN BE USED IN ALMOST ANY MEAL. ADD YOUR FAVOURITE SAUCE AND THEY STAND TALL.

CAVATELLI: Made from 2–3 cm (¾–1¼ inch) pieces of dough pressed and pushed with the thumb to make a curved and slightly hollowed oval shape. It is ideal with vegetable sauces, rich tomato sauces and seafood. Replace with orecchiette, pasta gnocchi or sardi (not shown).

Conchiglie (shells): There are three sizes.

CONCHIGLIE is the most common of the shell pastas and is of a medium size with a ribbed surface that collects a lot of sauce. You can use pasta gnocchi or orecchiette instead.

CONCHIGLIETTE is the smallest; usually used in soups. Substitute ditalini or stelline (not shown).

CONCHIGLIONE is the largest and is often stuffed .

DITALINI: One of several tiny pasta shapes that are mainly used in soups, ditalini is a tiny tube-shaped pasta that can either have a smooth or ribbed surface. You can use any of the tiny pastas, such as the little star pasta, stelline (not shown), or orzo.

FARFALLE: The name means butterfly in Italian, which refers to its pretty shape. It is best with thick or chunky sauces, which catch in the folds. You can also use a similar-sized pasta, such as fusilli or penne.

MACARONI: Very similar to elbow macaroni but without the curve. Macaroni, otherwise known as straight macaroni, is a small tube pasta usually used in soups and bakes. The best substitute is elbow macaroni; you can also use cotelli or garganelli .

ORECCHIETTE: Orecchiette means little ears in Italian, and the name of the pasta is a typically literal description of the shape – although some brands look more like curls than ears. It is best with thick or chunky sauces. You can substitute cavatelli, conchiglie or pasta gnocchi.

ORZO: In Italian, orzo means barley and the pasta is so-called because of its similarity in appearance to grains of barley. It is mainly used in clear soups, but it can also be used as a substitute for rice in risotto. It is a little bigger than risoni.

PASTA GNOCCHI: Not to be confused with the potato dumplings of the same name, pasta gnocchi is, as the name suggests, a pasta of a similar shape to potato gnocchi. The curves of the pasta make is especially suitable to being served with thick or chunky sauces. Some suitable replacements are cavatelli, conchiglie or orecchiette.

PENNE: A popular quill-shaped tube, sometimes ribbed and sometimes plain. It is usually about 4 cm (1½ inch) long. It is best with thick or chunky sauces. You can replace it with a pasta of a similar size, such as fusilli, garganelli, passatelli (not shown), or rigatoni.

RIGATONI: There are many sizes of this tube-shaped pasta. The largest size is usually stuffed and baked, but the other sizes are all interchangeable. The ribbed walls of the pasta catch the sauce. You can substitute large fusilli, penne or rotelle.

RISONI: This is a small pasta that looks very similar to arborio rice. It is best used in soups, bakes and casseroles or when used in a risotto instead of rice.

CAVATELLI   CONCHIGLIE   DITALINI   FARFALLE   MACARONI

Stelline (not shown), orzo or ditalini will work well in the same recipes (but not in risotto).

ROTELLE: Otherwise known as ruote, this pasta has a very distinctive wheel shape. Traditionally it is served with a tomato sauce, but it is suitable for most sauces. If you need to replace it, use a pasta of similar size, such as cresti di gallo, farfalle or rigatoni.

CURLY

THE CURLS AND SWIRLS OF CURLY PASTA SHAPES ADD INTEREST TO EVEN THE SIMPLEST OF SAUCES. THE CHALLENGE IS CATCHING THEM WITH YOUR FORK!

COTELLI: Otherwise known as cavatappi, these hollow tubes of pasta are formed into curls or ringlets. Cotelli is best with thick or chunky sauces as the chunks of the sauce get caught up in the curls. You can substitute a similar-sized and shaped pasta, such as cresti di gallo, elbow macaroni or fusilli.

CRESTI DI GALLO: Named after the Italian word for 'cockscombs', the name of this pasta is a reference to the similarity in shape to the crest of a rooster. Its basic structure is similar to elbow macaroni with the addition of a ruffled frill on the outside edge of the pasta. It can be replaced by rotelle or cotelli.

ELBOW MACARONI: The name elbow macaroni is an American term for short curved hollow tubes of pasta. It is part of the macaroni family, with a curve in the middle. Elbow macaroni is usually eaten with sauces based on meat, sausages and tomato. The closest substitutes for elbow macaroni are straight macaroni, cotelli or garganelli.

FRICELLI: These small tubes of pasta are formed into pretty spirals. They are not always readily available, but you can substitute cavatelli, penne, fusilli or garganelli.

FUSILLI: This corkscrew-shaped pasta can range in size from 4 to 30 cm (1½ to 12 inch) long; we have used pieces that are about 4 cm (1½ inch). Fusilli is most often available in dried form. It is commonly served with meat dishes and simple tomato sauces. You can replace fusilli with farfalle, penne, cotelli or garganelli.

GARGANELLI: This pasta is made with an egg dough that has grated Parmesan and nutmeg added to it. The outside surface of garganelli is ribbed. The ribs are formed by cutting the pasta into 4 cm (1½ inch) squares, wrapping the squares around a conical tool, then pressing them onto a ribbed wooden block. Garganelli is commonly served in a broth or with Bolognese sauce but is suitable for a wide range of pasta sauces. Penne, fricelli or fusilli can all be substituted for garganelli.

LONG

FRESH OR DRIED, LONG PASTA MAY NOT BE THE TIDIEST OF MEALS, BUT THE SENSATION OF EATING THE THIN STRANDS MAKES IT ALL WORTHWHILE.

ANGEL HAIR PASTA: Also called capelli d'angelo, this pasta is only available in dried form and it is the thinnest of all the spaghetti pastas. Resembling strands of long, blonde hair, its fine texture is best suited for use in broths and with extremely delicate, light, smooth sauces. Angel hair pasta can be replaced with capellini (not shown), spaghettini or vermicelli.

BUCATINI: Similar to thick spaghetti but with a hollow centre that helps it cook more quickly than spaghetti.

FRICELLI

FUSILLI

GARGANELLI

ANGEL HAIR PASTA

BUCATINI

Bucatini means small hole in Italian. It is traditionally served with carbonara and Amatriciana sauces. You can substitute linguine, spaghetti or one of the longer fusilli pastas for bucatini.

FETTUCINE: This pasta is slightly narrower and thicker than the very similar pasta, tagliatelle. It is usually served with rich, creamy sauces or simple fresh flavours, because the thickness of the strands helps it to carry the accompanying sauce. You can use trenette (not shown) or tagliatelle instead. There are several varieties of this very popular pasta; we have used only a few of the many types available.

Fresh spinach fettucine: Also known as fettucine verde due to its rich green colour, it is made by the addition of cooked, well-drained spinach to the dough before it is kneaded. The most popular of the coloured pastas, its colour makes it an attractive companion to both red tomato-based sauces and white cream-based ones.

LINGUINE (fresh, dried): The Italian word for 'little tongues', linguine is a long flat pasta also known as bavette. It is good with pesto or seafood sauces. Substitute bucatini, fettucine, spaghetti, tagliatelle or long fusilli, remembering that if the recipe asks for fresh pasta, use fresh and if it asks for dried, use dried.

SPAGHETTI (fresh, dried): The name of this very popular pasta comes from the Italian word 'strings'. Nowadays, spaghetti is made all over the world. The commercial making of spaghetti involves pushing the pasta dough through an extrusion system to make the noodles. Out of all the hundreds of pasta shapes, spaghetti is the most versatile. It is suitable for a large number of sauces and it comes in 2–3 different thicknesses, one being thin spaghetti, also known as spaghettini. Substitute bucatini or spaghettini. Always replace fresh pasta with fresh and dried pasta with dried.

SPAGHETTINI: Very similar to spaghetti, but even thinner, these so-called 'little lengths of cord' make an ideal match for delicate, oil-based sauces such as the Italian classic aglio e olio (garlic and olive oil) or fish and shellfish sauces. Spaghettini is often only available as dried pasta. Substitute other long, fine pastas such as angel hair pasta, spaghetti or vermicelli.

TAGLIATELLE (fresh, dried): Slightly wider than fettucine, these very thin, flat ribbon noodles are the northern Italian name for fettucine. In fact, the two are interchangeable. Tagliatelle, not spaghetti, is the traditional accompaniment to Bolognese sauce. Unlike other pasta shapes, both fresh and dried tagliatelle are made with the addition of egg to the pasta dough. Like other ribbon pastas, it is at its best when accompanied by light cream or butter-based sauces, or fresh flavours. You can substitute lasagnette or fettucine.

VERMICELLI: Meaning 'little worms' in Italian, it is a very fine, long pasta best eaten in broth-based noodle soups or with fine-textured tomato, butter or cheese sauces which cling well to its length. Vermicelli is thinner than spaghetti. Replace with spaghettini or angel hair pasta.

ZITI: A long, tubular pasta, its strong, thick texture and hollow interior are excellent for picking up heavy meat sauces such as ragus and chunky vegetable sauces. Unlike other long pastas, it is often broken into smaller pieces prior to cooking. It can be replaced with pasta of a similar size like candele (not shown), lasagnette, rigatoni, penne or bucatini.

FETTUCINE

LINGUINE

SPAGHETTI

SPAGHETTINI

TAGLIATELLE

VERMICELLI

ZITI

AGNOLOTTI

CONCHIGLIONE

RAVIOLI

FILLED

LIKE A CAREFULLY CHOSEN PRESENT, FILLED PASTA IS AS GOOD ON THE INSIDE AS ON THE OUTSIDE. A DELECTABLE FILLING IS ENCLOSED BY A PASTA WRAPPING PERFECT IN ITS SIMPLICITY.

AGNOLOTTI: The name for filled pasta in the Piedmont region of Italy, agnolotti can be shaped into squares, crescents or circles, and usually have ruffled edges. Agnolotti was originally used to wrap up leftovers of meat and sausage in fresh pasta.

CONCHIGLIONE (large shells): Part of the conchiglie (shell) family of pasta, conchiglione is the largest of the shells. It is usually stuffed with a filling and baked in a ceramic dish: its shape makes it a natural for stuffing as the hollow centre is excellent for holding cheese, meat or seafood and sauce. It can be substituted with other large pasta shapes including large rigatoni or lumaconi, the giant pasta snails (not shown).

RAVIOLI: The most recognised filled pasta outside Italy, ravioli are little stuffed square pasta pillows.

TORTELLINI: Originating in Bologna, these small pasta rings are said to be named after Venus' navel. There are several popular fillings.

FLAT

NOT CONTENT TO BE THE POOR RELATION, FLAT PASTA MAKES ITS BIGGEST IMPACT BY LAYERING SHEETS OF PASTA WITH A DELICIOUS FILLING. LASAGNE IS ALWAYS A FAVOURITE, BUT IT IS ONLY ONE OF MANY MOUTH-WATERING OPTIONS USING FLAT PASTA.

DRIED LASAGNE: Dried lasagne sheets are readily available from the supermarket and are best cooked as their packet instructions indicate. These large sheets of dried pasta are used for making baked, layered pasta dishes and are increasingly being used for free-form pasta stacks.

LASAGNETTE: Also called mafalde or mafaldini, these wide, long fluted lengths of pasta have slightly crimped edges ideal for catching their accompanying sauce. Lasagnette is best matched with rich meat, vegetable, cream or cheese sauces. It is usually available

dried, not fresh. If you can't find it, use another dried pasta of a similar length and width, such as pappardelle.

DRIED PAPPARDELLE: These dried, very wide pasta ribbons are different to most other dried pastas as their dough is enriched with eggs, which is quite unusual for a dried pasta. Their width and length are best matched with strong sauces that will cover their entire surface area. You can replace dried pappardelle with dried tagliatelle or lasagnette, but unless you are using an egg pasta, they will not have quite the same flavour.

STRACCI: Made from fresh pasta sheets, stracci, meaning 'stretched' in Italian, is one of the easiest pasta shapes to make. Large pasta sheets are simply sliced into reasonably large and varied shapes by cutting different lengths along a range of angles. Stracci can be substituted quite easily by breaking dried lasagne sheets into ragged pieces about 7 x 12 cm (2¾ x 5 inch). Any sauce that goes with stracci will also go well with fresh or dried fettucine or tagliatelle. Stracci is most often available dried.

TORTELLINI

LASAGNE

LASAGNETTE

PAPPARDELLE

STRACCI

Roasted Orange Sweet Potato and Ditalini Patties

PREPARATION TIME: 15 minutes
COOKING TIME: 1 hour 10 minutes
SERVES 4

2 orange sweet potatoes
  (about 800 g/1 lb 12 oz in total)
90 g (½ cup) ditalini
30 g (1 oz) toasted pine nuts
2 garlic cloves, crushed
4 tablespoons finely chopped basil
50 g (½ cup) grated Parmesan cheese
35 g (⅓ cup) dry breadcrumbs
plain (all-purpose) flour, for dusting
olive oil, for shallow-frying

1 Preheat the oven to 250°C (500°F/Gas 10). Pierce the whole orange sweet potatoes several times with a fork, then place in a roasting tin and roast for about 1 hour, or until soft. Remove from the oven and cool. Meanwhile, cook the pasta in a large saucepan of boiling water until al dente. Drain and rinse under running water.

2 Peel the sweet potato and mash the flesh with a potato masher or fork, then add the pine nuts, garlic, basil, Parmesan, breadcrumbs and the pasta and combine. Season.

3 Shape the mixture into eight even patties (about 1.5 cm/⅝ inch thick) with floured hands, then lightly dust the patties with flour. Heat the oil in a large frying pan and cook the patties in batches over medium heat for 2 minutes each side, or until golden and heated through. Drain on crumpled paper towels, sprinkle with salt and serve immediately. Great with a fresh green salad.

Pierce the sweet potatoes several times with a sharp knife.

When roasted, peel the sweet potatoes and mash the flesh.

Form sweet potato mixture into patties and dust with flour.

Tomato Ditalini Soup

PREPARATION TIME: 15 minutes
COOKING TIME: 20 minutes
SERVES 4

2 tablespoons olive oil
1 large onion, finely chopped
2 celery sticks, finely chopped
3 vine-ripened tomatoes
1.5 litres (6 cups) chicken or vegetable stock
90 g (½ cup) ditalini
2 tablespoons chopped fresh
  flat-leaf (Italian) parsley

1 Heat the oil in a large saucepan over medium heat. Add the onion and celery and cook for 5 minutes, or until they have softened.

2 Score a cross in the base of each tomato, then place in a bowl of boiling water for 1 minute. Plunge into cold water and peel the skin away from the cross. Halve the tomatoes and scoop out the seeds. Roughly chop the flesh. Add the stock and tomato to the onion mixture and bring to the boil. Add the pasta and cook for 10 minutes, or until al dente. Season and sprinkle with parsley.

Cook onion and celery over medium heat until soft.

Scoop seed from tomatoes and chop the flesh.

Pasta e Fagioli (Hearty Pasta and Bean Soup)

PREPARATION TIME: 15 minutes

COOKING TIME: 20 minutes

SERVES 4

1 tablespoon olive oil
1 onion, finely chopped
3 garlic cloves, crushed
2 x 290 g (10 oz) cans mixed beans, drained
1.75 litres (7 cups) chicken stock
100 g (3½ oz) conchigliette
1 tablespoon chopped fresh tarragon

1 Heat the oil in a saucepan over low heat. Add the onion and cook for 5 minutes, then add the garlic and cook for a further 1 minute, stirring frequently. Add the beans and chicken stock, cover the pan with a lid, increase the heat and bring to the boil. Add the pasta and cook until al dente. Stir in the tarragon, then season with salt and ground black pepper. Serve with crusty bread.

Cook onion and garlic over low heat, then add beans and stock.

Crab, Camembert and Fusilli Frittata

PREPARATION TIME: 15 minutes
COOKING TIME: 50 minutes
SERVES 4–6

80 g (1 cup) tri-coloured fusilli
1 tablespoon olive oil
1 very small red onion, finely chopped
1 large Roma (plum) tomato, roughly chopped
60 g (⅓ cup) semi-dried (sun-blushed) tomatoes, roughly chopped
2 tablespoons finely chopped fresh coriander (cilantro) leaves
140 g (⅔ cup) cooked fresh or canned crab meat
150 g (5½ oz) Camembert cheese, rind removed, cut into small pieces
6 eggs plus 2 egg yolks

1 Cook the pasta in a large saucepan of boiling water until al dente. Drain, rinse, then drain again and set aside to cool. Meanwhile, heat half the oil in a small frying pan over low heat, add the onion and cook for 4–5 minutes, or until softened but not browned. Transfer to a bowl and add the Roma tomato, semi-dried tomatoes and coriander. Squeeze out any excess moisture from the crab meat and add the meat to the bowl. Add half the cheese to the bowl, then add the cooled pasta. Mix well. Beat together the six eggs and the two extra yolks, then stir into the tomato and crab mixture. Season.

2 Heat the remaining oil in the frying pan, pour in the frittata mixture and cook over low heat for 25 minutes. Preheat the grill (broiler) to low. Scatter the remaining Camembert over the frittata before placing it under the grill for 10–15 minutes, or until cooked and golden brown on top. Remove from the grill and leave for 5 minutes. Cut into slices and serve with salad and bread.

Ensure pasta has cooled before adding to other ingredients.

Scatter remaining Camembert over frittata; grill (broil) until golden.

Warm Chicken and Pasta Salad

PREPARATION TIME: 15 minutes
COOKING TIME: 15 minutes
SERVES 4

375 g (13 oz) penne
100 ml (3½ fl oz) olive oil
4 slender eggplants (aubergines),
  thinly sliced on the diagonal
2 chicken breast fillets
2 teaspoons lemon juice
15 g (½ cup) chopped fresh
  flat-leaf (Italian) parsley
270 g (9¾ oz) chargrilled red capsicum
  (pepper), drained and sliced
155 g (5½ oz) fresh asparagus, trimmed,
  blanched and cut into 5 cm (2 inch)
  lengths
85 g (3 oz) semi-dried (sun-blushed) tomatoes, finely sliced

1 Cook the pasta in a large saucepan of boiling water until al dente. Drain, return to the pan and keep warm. Heat 2 tablespoons of the oil in a large frying pan over high heat and cook the eggplant for 4–5 minutes, or until golden and cooked through.

2 Heat a lightly oiled chargrill pan (griddle) over high heat and cook the chicken for 5 minutes each side, or until browned and cooked through. Cut into thick slices. Put the lemon juice, parsley and remaining oil in a small jar and shake well. Return the pasta to the heat, toss through the dressing, chicken, eggplant, capsicum, asparagus and tomato until well mixed and warmed through. Season with black pepper. Serve warm with grated Parmesan, if desired.

Cook eggplant over high heat until golden and cooked through.

Cook chicken over high heat for 5 minutes each size until browned.

Spaghetti With Shellfish and White Wine Sauce

PREPARATION TIME: 15 minutes
COOKING TIME: 10 minutes
SERVES 4

500 g (1 lb 2 oz) mussels
1 kg (2 lb 4 oz) clams (vongoles)
400 g (14 oz) fresh spaghetti
2 tablespoons olive oil
4 French shallots, finely chopped
2 garlic cloves, crushed
250 ml (1 cup) dry white wine
3 tablespoons chopped fresh
   flat-leaf (Italian) parsley

1 Scrub the mussels with a stiff brush and remove any barnacles with a knife. Remove the beards. Discard any mussels or clams that are broken or open ones that do not close when tapped on the work surface. Wash them both thoroughly under cold running water. Cook the pasta in a large saucepan of boiling water until al dente. Drain and keep warm in a large saucepan.

2 Meanwhile, heat the oil in a large saucepan over medium heat and cook the shallots for 4 minutes, or until softened. Add the garlic and cook for a further 1 minute. Pour in the wine, bring to the boil and cook for 2 minutes, or until reduced slightly. Add the clams and mussels, tossing to coat them in the liquid, then cover the pan. Cook, shaking the pan regularly, for about 3 minutes, or until the shells have opened. Discard any clams or mussels that do not open. Toss the clam mixture through the spaghetti, scatter with parsley and transfer to a warmed serving dish. Season and serve with salad and bread.

Scrub mussels and remove beards, discarding any that are broken.

Cook mussels and clams in wine mixture until shells have opened.

Penne with Veal Ragout

PREPARATION TIME: 15 minutes
COOKING TIME: 2 hours 40 minutes
SERVES 4

2 onions, sliced
2 bay leaves, crushed
1.5 kg (3 lb 5 oz) veal shin, cut into osso
   bucco pieces
250 ml (1 cup) red wine
2 x 400 g (14 oz) cans crushed tomatoes
375 ml (1½ cups) beef stock
2 teaspoons chopped fresh rosemary
400 g (14 oz) penne
140 g (1 cup) frozen peas

1 Preheat oven to 220°C (425°F/Gas 7). Scatter the onion over bottom of a large roasting tin (we used 32 x 23 cm/13 x 9 inch), lightly spray with oil and place the bay leaves and veal pieces on top. Season. Roast for 10–15 minutes, or until the veal is browned. Ensure the onion doesn't burn.

2 Pour wine over the veal and return to oven for a further 5 minutes. Reduce heat to 180°C (350°F/Gas 4), remove tin from oven and pour on the tomato, stock and 1 teaspoon of the rosemary. Cover with foil and return to oven. Cook for 2 hours, or until veal is starting to fall from bone. Remove foil and cook for a further 15 minutes, or until the meat loosens away from the bone and the liquid has evaporated slightly.

3 Cook pasta in a large saucepan of boiling water until al dente. Meanwhile, remove veal from oven and cool slightly. Add peas and remaining rosemary and place over a hotplate. Cook over medium heat for 5 minutes, or until peas are cooked. Drain pasta, divide among four bowls and top with the ragout.

Roast the veal pieces in a medium hot oven until well browned.

Add tomato, stock and rosemary and cook for a further 2 hours.

Add peas and remaining rosemary and cook until peas are tender.

Pasta di Stalla (Pasta from the Barn)

PREPARATION TIME: 10 minutes
COOKING TIME: 15 minutes
SERVES 4

375 g (13 oz) orecchiette
1 large potato, cut into 1.5 cm
 (⅝ inch) cubes
400 g (14 oz) broccoli
80 ml (⅓ cup) olive oil
3 garlic cloves, crushed
1 small red chilli, finely chopped
2 x 400 g (14 oz) cans chopped tomatoes
25 g (¼ cup) grated pecorino cheese

1 Bring a large saucepan of salted water to the boil and cook the pasta and potato for 8–10 minutes, or until the pasta is al dente. Drain and return to the pan. Meanwhile, trim the broccoli into florets and discard the stems. Place in a saucepan of boiling water and cook for 1–2 minutes, then drain and plunge into iced water. Drain and add to the pasta and potato.

2 Heat the oil in a saucepan, add the garlic and chilli and cook for 30 seconds. Add the tomato and simmer for 5 minutes, or until slightly reduced and thickened. Season to taste with salt and pepper.

3 Pour the tomato mixture over the pasta, potato and broccoli. Toss well and stir over low heat until warmed through. Serve sprinkled with grated pecorino cheese.

Cook broccoli florets briefly then plunge into iced water.

Simmer tomato, garlic and chilli for 5 minutes, until slightly thickened.

Pour tomato mixture over pasta, potato and broccoli, and toss well.

Linguine with Ham, Artichoke and Lemon Sauce

PREPARATION TIME: 15 minutes
COOKING TIME: 10 minutes
SERVES 4

500 g (1 lb 2 oz) fresh linguine
25 g (1 oz) butter
2 large garlic cloves, chopped
150 g (5½ oz) marinated artichokes,
  drained and quartered
150 g (5½ oz) sliced leg ham, cut into strips
300 ml (10½ fl oz) cream
2 teaspoons coarsely grated lemon zest
15 g (½ cup) fresh basil, torn
35 g (⅓ cup) grated Parmesan cheese

1 Cook the pasta in a large saucepan of boiling water until al dente. Drain, then return to the pan. Meanwhile, melt the butter in a large frying pan, add the garlic and cook over medium heat for 1 minute, or until fragrant. Add the artichokes and ham and cook for a further 2 minutes.

2 Add the cream and lemon zest, reduce the heat and simmer for 5 minutes, gently breaking up the artichokes with a spoon. Pour the sauce over the pasta, then add the basil and Parmesan and toss until the pasta is evenly coated. Divide among four serving plates and serve.

Cook garlic, then add artichokes and ham and cook for 2 minutes.

Add the cream and lemon zest to artichoke mixture, and simmer.

Risoni Risotto with Mushrooms and Pancetta

PREPARATION TIME: 15 minutes
COOKING TIME: 35 minutes
SERVES 4–6

25 g (1 oz) butter
2 garlic cloves, finely chopped
150 g (5½ oz) piece pancetta, diced
400 g (14 oz) button mushrooms, sliced
500 g (1 lb 2 oz) risoni
1 litre (4 cups) chicken stock
125 ml (½ cup) cream
50 g (½ cup) finely grated Parmesan cheese
4 tablespoons finely chopped fresh flat-leaf (Italian) parsley

1 Melt the butter in a saucepan, add the garlic and cook over medium heat for 30 seconds, then increase the heat to high, add the pancetta and cook for 3–5 minutes, or until crisp. Add the mushrooms and cook for 3–5 minutes, or until softened.

2 Add the risoni, stir until coated in the mixture. Add the stock and bring to the boil. Reduce the heat to medium and cook, covered, for 15–20 minutes, or until nearly all the liquid has evaporated and the risoni is tender.

3 Stir in the cream and cook, uncovered, for a further 3 minutes, stirring occasionally until the cream is absorbed. Stir in 35 g (⅓ cup) of the Parmesan and all the parsley and season to taste. Divide among four serving bowls and serve sprinkled with the remaining Parmesan.

Cook pancetta over high heat for 3–5 minutes, until crisp.

Add risoni, then stock, and cook until liquid has evaporated.

Stir in the Parmesan and parsley and season to taste.

Spaghetti With Herb, Garlic and Chilli Oil

PREPARATION TIME: 15 minutes
COOKING TIME: 15 minutes
SERVES 4–6

250 ml (1 cup) good-quality olive oil
2 bird's eye chillies, seeded and thinly sliced
5–6 large cloves garlic, crushed
500 g (1 lb 2 oz) spaghetti
100 g (3½ oz) thinly sliced prosciutto
30 g (½ cup) chopped fresh flat-leaf (Italian) parsley
2 tablespoons chopped fresh basil
2 tablespoons chopped fresh oregano
75 g (¾ cup) good-quality grated Parmesan cheese

1 Pour the oil into a small saucepan with the chilli and garlic. Slowly heat the oil over low heat for about 12 minutes to infuse the oil with the garlic and chilli. Don't allow the oil to reach smoking point or the garlic will burn and taste bitter.

2 Meanwhile, cook the pasta in a large saucepan of boiling water until al dente. Drain well and return to the pan. Lay the prosciutto on a grill (broiler) tray and cook under a hot grill for 2 minutes each side, or until crispy. Cool and break into pieces.

3 Pour the hot oil mixture over the spaghetti and toss well with the prosciutto, fresh herbs and Parmesan. Season to taste.

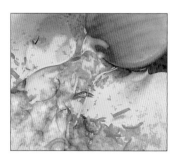

Heat oil over low heat, allowing garlic and chilli to infuse the oil.

Cook prosciutto under grill (broiler) until crispy.

Pour oil mixture over cooked pasta and toss prosciutto through.

Pasta Gnocchi with Sausage and Tomato

PREPARATION TIME: 15 minutes
COOKING TIME: 20 minutes
SERVES 4–6

500 g (1 lb 2 oz) pasta gnocchi
2 tablespoons olive oil
400 g (14 oz) thin Italian sausages
1 red onion, finely chopped
2 garlic cloves, finely chopped
2 x 400 g (14 oz) cans chopped tomatoes
1 teaspoon caster (superfine) sugar
35 g (1¼ oz) fresh basil, torn
45 g (½ cup) grated pecorino cheese

1 Cook the pasta in a large saucepan of boiling water until al dente. Drain and return the pasta to the pan. Meanwhile, heat 2 teaspoons of the oil in a large frying pan. Add the sausages and cook, turning, for 5 minutes, or until well browned and cooked through. Drain on paper towels, then slice when they have cooled enough to touch. Keep warm.

2 Wipe clean the frying pan and heat the remaining oil. Add the onion and garlic and cook over medium heat for 2 minutes, or until the onion has softened. Add the tomato, sugar and 250 ml (1 cup) water and season well with ground black pepper. Reduce the heat and simmer for 12 minutes, or until thickened and reduced a little.

3 Pour the sauce over the cooked pasta and stir through the sausage, then the basil and half of the cheese. Divide among serving plates and serve hot with the remaining cheese sprinkled over the top.

Cook sausages until browned; when cool, slice into pieces.

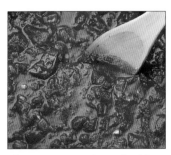

Simmer tomato mixture for 12 minutes, until thickened.

Pour sauce over cooked pasta and stir through sausage pieces.

Linguine with Broccoli, Pine Nuts and Lemon

PREPARATION TIME: 15 minutes
COOKING TIME: 15 minutes
SERVES 4–6

500 g (1 lb 2 oz) linguine
600 g (1 lb 5 oz) broccoli, cut into small florets
80 g (½ cup) pine nuts
125 ml (½ cup) extra virgin olive oil
2 teaspoons finely grated lemon zest
60 ml (¼ cup) lemon juice
1 teaspoon dried chilli flakes
50 g (½ cup) finely grated good-quality Parmesan cheese

1 Cook the pasta in a large saucepan of boiling water until al dente. Drain and return to the pan. Meanwhile, bring a saucepan of water to the boil and cook the broccoli for 2 minutes, or until just tender but still bright green. Drain and set aside.

2 Heat a large non-stick frying pan and toast the pine nuts for 2–3 minutes, or until just golden, shaking the pan to prevent them burning. Remove from the pan and roughly chop. Reduce the heat to low, add the oil and lemon zest to the frying pan and gently heat until fragrant. Add the broccoli, chopped nuts, lemon juice and chilli and stir until warmed through. Season. Add to the pasta with the Parmesan and toss to combine. Divide among serving bowls and serve.

Cook pasta in large saucepan of boiling water until al dente.

Stir together broccoli, pine nuts, lemon juice and chilli.

Penne with Pumpkin, Baked Ricotta and Prosciutto

PREPARATION TIME: 15 minutes
COOKING TIME: 15 minutes
SERVES 4

500 g (1 lb 2 oz) penne
460 g (1 lb) butternut pumpkin (squash),
   cut in 1 cm (½ inch) cubes
60 ml (¼ cup) extra virgin olive oil
2 garlic cloves, crushed
100 g (3½ oz) semi-dried (sun-blushed)
   tomatoes, chopped
4 slices prosciutto, chopped
250 g (9 oz) baked ricotta cheese, cut into
   1 cm (½ inch) cubes
3 tablespoons shredded fresh basil

1 Cook the pasta in a large saucepan of boiling water until al dente. Drain. Meanwhile, cook the pumpkin in a saucepan of boiling water for 10–12 minutes, or until just tender, then drain well.

2 Heat the oil in a large saucepan, add the garlic and cook over medium heat for 30 seconds. Add the tomato, prosciutto, pumpkin and penne and toss gently over low heat for 1–2 minutes, or until heated through.

3 Add the baked ricotta and the basil, season and serve immediately.

Cook pumpkin until just tender and drain well.

Toss together tomato, prosciutto, pumpkin and penne over low heat.

Add ricotta and basil, season, and serve.

Angel Hair Pasta with Creamy Garlic Prawns

PREPARATION TIME: 15 minutes
COOKING TIME: 15 minutes
SERVES 4

2 tablespoons olive oil
16 raw medium prawns (shrimp), peeled
1 leek, chopped
6 garlic cloves, crushed
½ teaspoon dried chilli flakes
125 ml (½ cup) dry white wine
200 ml (7 fl oz) cream
250 g (9 oz) angel hair pasta
3 tablespoons chopped fresh
   flat-leaf (Italian) parsley

1 Heat half the oil in a frying pan and season the prawns. Add to the pan and cook over high heat for 2–3 minutes, or until cooked. Remove from the pan, cover and keep warm.

2 Heat the remaining oil in the same pan, add the leek and cook, stirring, over medium heat for 2–3 minutes, or until softened. Add the garlic and chilli flakes and stir for 1 minute. Pour in the wine, reduce the heat and simmer for 4 minutes, or until reduced. Add the cream and simmer for 3 minutes, or until just thickened.

3 Meanwhile, cook the pasta in a large saucepan of boiling water until al dente. Drain and return to the pan. Stir the parsley into the sauce and season well. Add to the pasta and stir to coat. Divide among the serving bowls and top with prawns.

Cook prawns over high heat, remove from pan and keep warm.

Cook garlic and chilli, add wine and simmer until reduced.

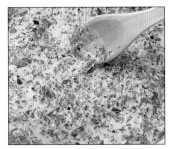
Add cream and simmer for 3 minutes until just thickened.

Farfalle with Spinach and Bacon

PREPARATION TIME: 10 minutes
COOKING TIME: 15 minutes
SERVES 4

400 g (14 oz) farfalle
2 tablespoons extra virgin olive oil
250 g (9 oz) bacon, chopped
1 red onion, finely chopped
250 g (9 oz) baby English spinach leaves,
  stalks trimmed
1–2 tablespoons sweet chilli sauce (optional)
35 g (¼ cup) crumbled goat's feta cheese

1 Cook the pasta in a large saucepan of boiling water until al dente, then drain and return to the saucepan. Meanwhile, heat the oil in a frying pan, add the bacon and cook over medium heat for 3 minutes, or until golden. Add the onion and cook for a further 4 minutes, or until softened. Toss the spinach leaves through the onion and bacon mixture for 30 seconds, or until just wilted.

2 Add the bacon and spinach mixture to the drained pasta, then stir in the sweet chilli sauce. Season to taste with salt and ground black pepper and toss well. Spoon into warm bowls and scatter with the crumbled feta. Serve immediately.

*Cook bacon over medium heat for
3 minutes, until golden.*

*Add bacon and spinach mixture
to pasta, then stir in chilli sauce.*

Creamy Pasta Gnocchi with Peas and Prosciutto

PREPARATION TIME: 15 minutes
COOKING TIME: 20 minutes
SERVES 4

100 g (3½ oz) thinly sliced prosciutto
3 teaspoons oil
2 eggs
250 ml (1 cup) cream
35 g (⅓ cup) grated Parmesan cheese
2 tablespoons chopped fresh
   flat-leaf (Italian) parsley
1 tablespoon chopped fresh chives
250 g (9 oz) fresh or frozen peas
500 g (1 lb 2 oz) pasta gnocchi

1 Cut the prosciutto into 5 mm (¼ inch) wide strips. Heat the oil in a frying pan over medium heat, cook the prosciutto for 2 minutes, or until crisp. Drain on paper towels. Place the eggs, cream, Parmesan and herbs in a bowl and whisk well.

2 Bring a large saucepan of salted water to the boil. Add the peas and cook for 5 minutes, or until just tender. Leaving the pan on the heat, use a slotted spoon and transfer the peas to the bowl of cream mixture, and then add 60 ml (¼ cup) of the cooking liquid to the same bowl. Using a potato masher or the back of a fork, roughly mash the peas.

3 Add the gnocchi to the boiling water and cook until al dente. Drain well, then return to the pan. Add the cream mixture, then warm through over low heat, gently stirring for about 30 seconds until the gnocchi is coated in the sauce. Season. Divide among warmed plates, top with the prosciutto and serve immediately.

Cook prosciutto strips over medium heat until crisp.

Whisk together eggs, cream, Parmesan and herbs.

Add cream mixture to cooked gnocchi and stir through gently.

Rotelle with Chickpeas, Tomato and Parsley

PREPARATION TIME: 10 minutes
COOKING TIME: 15 minutes
SERVES 4

375 g (13 oz) rotelle
1 tablespoon ground cumin
125 ml (½ cup) olive oil
1 red onion, halved and thinly sliced
3 garlic cloves, crushed
400 g (14 oz) can chickpeas, drained
3 large tomatoes, diced
15 g (½ cup) chopped fresh flat-leaf (Italian)
   parsley
60 ml (¼ cup) lemon juice

1 Cook the pasta in a large saucepan of boiling water until al dente. Drain and return to the pan.

2 Meanwhile, heat a large frying pan over medium heat, add the cumin and cook, tossing, for 1 minute, or until fragrant. Remove from the pan. Heat half the oil in the same pan and cook the onion over medium heat for 2–3 minutes, or until soft. Stir in the garlic, chickpeas, tomato and parsley and stir until warmed through. Gently toss through the pasta.

3 Place the lemon juice, cumin and remaining oil in a jar with a lid and shake together well. Add the dressing to the saucepan with the pasta and chickpea mixture, return to the stove-top over low heat and stir until warmed through. Season well with salt and ground black pepper. Serve hot with grated Parmesan, or you can serve it cold. If serving cold, rinse the pasta under cold water before adding the chickpea mixture and do not return to the heat.

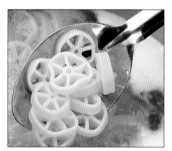
Cook rotelle in a large saucepan of boiling water until al dente.

Cook onion, then add garlic, chickpeas, tomato and parsley.

Combine lemon juice, cumin and oil in a jar, and pour over pasta.

Penne with Rustic Lentil Sauce

PREPARATION TIME: 10 minutes
COOKING TIME: 30 minutes
SERVES 4

1 litre (4 cups) chicken stock
350 g (12 oz) penne
80 ml (⅓ cup) virgin olive oil, plus extra for
  drizzling
1 onion, chopped
2 carrots, diced
3 celery sticks, diced
3 garlic cloves, crushed
1 tablespoon plus 1 teaspoon chopped fresh
  thyme
400 g (14 oz) can lentils, drained

1 Boil the chicken stock in a large saucepan for 10 minutes, or until reduced to 500 ml (2 cups) of liquid. Meanwhile, cook the pasta in a large saucepan of boiling water until al dente. Drain and toss with 2 tablespoons of the olive oil.

2 Heat the remaining oil in a large, deep frying pan, add the onion, carrot and celery and cook over medium heat for 10 minutes, or until browned. Add two thirds of the crushed garlic and 1 tablespoon of the thyme and cook for a further 1 minute. Add the stock, bring to the boil and cook for 8 minutes, or until reduced slightly and the vegetables are tender. Gently stir in the lentils until heated through.

3 Stir in the remaining garlic and thyme, and season with plenty of salt and ground black pepper—the stock should be slightly syrupy at this point. Combine the pasta with the lentil sauce in a large bowl, drizzle generously with virgin olive oil and serve with grated Parmesan, if desired.

Toss cooked penne with 2 table-spoons olive oil.

Cook onion, carrot and celery over medium heat for 10 minutes.

Add thyme to stock and lentil sauce, along with salt and pepper.

Greek Pasta Salad

PREPARATION TIME: 10 minutes
COOKING TIME: 45 minutes
SERVES 4

4 Roma (plum) tomatoes, quartered
1 tablespoon chopped fresh oregano
500 g (1 lb 2 oz) rigatoni
250 g (9 oz) marinated soft feta cheese
1 red onion, halved and sliced
1 tablespoon capers in salt, rinsed and
   patted dry
2½ tablespoons red wine vinegar
15 g (½ cup) chopped fresh flat-leaf (Italian)
   parsley
2 tablespoons ready-made olive tapenade

1 Preheat the oven to 180°C (350°F/Gas 4). Place the tomatoes, cut-side-up, on a baking tray, sprinkle with 1 teaspoon of the oregano and season with salt and pepper. Roast for 30–40 minutes, or until soft and caramelized.

2 Meanwhile, cook the pasta in a large saucepan of boiling water until al dente. Drain the pasta and return to the pan to keep warm.

3 Drain and crumble the feta, reserving the oil and herbs. Heat 2 teaspoons of the reserved oil in a small frying pan, add the onion and cook over medium heat for 2–3 minutes, or until soft, then add the capers and cook for a further minute. Combine the rest of the reserved oil with the vinegar and stir into the pan. Remove from the heat and stir through the pasta, adding the remaining oregano and the parsley. Divide among four serving plates and top with the tomato, feta and the tapenade.

Sprinkle tomatoes with oregano and roast for 30–40 minutes.

Cook pasta in large saucepan of boiling water until al dente.

Combine oil and vinegar and stir into pan with onions and capers.

Rich Cheese Macaroni

PREPARATION TIME: 15 minutes
COOKING TIME: 40 minutes
SERVES 4

450 g (1 lb) elbow macaroni
40 g (1½ oz) butter
300 ml (10½ fl oz) cream
125 g (4½ oz) fontina cheese, sliced
125 g (4½ oz) provolone cheese, grated
100 g (3½ oz) Gruyère cheese, grated
125 g (4½ oz) blue castello cheese, crumbled
40 g (½ cup) fresh white breadcrumbs
25 g (¼ cup) grated Parmesan cheese

1 Preheat the oven to 180°C (350°F/Gas 4). Cook the pasta in a large saucepan of boiling water until al dente. Drain and keep warm. Melt half the butter in a large saucepan. Add the cream and, when just coming to the boil, add the fontina, provolone, Gruyère and blue castello cheeses, stirring constantly over low heat for 3 minutes, or until melted. Season with salt and ground white pepper. Add the pasta to the cheese mixture and mix well.

2 Spoon the mixture into a lightly greased shallow 2 litre (8 cup) ovenproof dish. Sprinkle with the breadcrumbs mixed with the Parmesan, dot with the remaining cubed butter and bake for 25 minutes, or until the top is golden and crisp. Serve with a salad.

Heat cream and cheeses over low heat for 3 minutes.

Add macaroni to cheese mixture and mix well.

Spaghetti Nicoise

PREPARATION TIME: 10 minutes
COOKING TIME: 15 minutes
SERVES 4–6

350 g (12 oz) spaghetti
8 quail eggs (or 4 hen eggs)
1 lemon
3 x 185 g (6¼ oz) cans good-quality
 tuna in oil
50 g (⅓ cup) pitted and halved
 Kalamata olives
100 g (3½ oz) semi-dried (sun-blushed)
 tomatoes, cut lengthways
4 anchovy fillets, chopped into small pieces
3 tablespoons baby capers, drained
3 tablespoons chopped fresh flat-leaf
 (Italian) parsley

1 Cook the pasta in a large saucepan of boiling water until al dente. Meanwhile, place the eggs in a saucepan of cold water, bring to the boil and cook for 4 minutes (10 minutes for hen eggs). Drain, cool under cold water, then peel. Cut the quail eggs into halves or the hen eggs into quarters. Finely grate the rind of the lemon to give 1 teaspoon of grated zest. Then, squeeze the lemon to give 2 tablespoons juice.

2 Empty the tuna and its oil into a large bowl. Add the olives, tomato halves, anchovies, lemon zest and juice, capers and 2 tablespoons of the parsley. Drain the pasta and rinse in a little cold water, then toss gently through the tuna mixture. Divide among serving bowls, garnish with egg and the extra chopped fresh parsley, and serve.

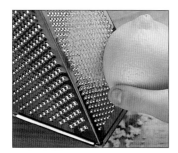

Finely grate the rind of a lemon to give 1 tablespoon grated zest.

Drain cooked pasta, rinse, and toss through tuna mixture.

Cotelli with Capers, Bocconcini and Basil Oil

PREPARATION TIME: 10 minutes
COOKING TIME: 15 minutes
SERVES 4–6

125 ml (½ cup) olive oil
125 g (4½ oz) jar capers in brine, drained
500 g (1 lb 2 oz) cotelli
2 tablespoons lemon juice
100 g (2 cups) firmly packed fresh basil
35 g (⅓ cup) grated Parmesan cheese
250 g (9 oz) cherry tomatoes, quartered
8 bocconcini cheese, quartered
extra virgin olive oil, for drizzling

1 Heat half the olive oil in a small pan, cook the capers over high heat for 3–4 minutes, or until crisp and golden. Drain on paper towels.

2 Cook the pasta in a large saucepan of boiling water until al dente. Drain and keep warm. Meanwhile, place the lemon juice, 75 g (1½ cups) of the basil and the remaining olive oil in a food processor and process until smooth. Season with salt and pepper.

3 Roughly tear the remaining basil leaves, then toss through the warm pasta with the basil mixture, 2 tablespoons of the Parmesan and the cherry tomatoes. Spoon into warmed bowls and top with the bocconcini and capers. Drizzle with extra virgin olive oil and garnish with the remaining grated Parmesan. Serve immediately.

Cook capers over high heat until crisp and golden.

Combine lemon juice, basil and olive oil and process until smooth.

Roughly tear remaining basil leaves and toss through pasta.

Smoked Chicken Linguine

PREPARATION TIME: 15 minutes
COOKING TIME: 20 minutes
SERVES 4

1 tablespoon olive oil
1 leek, thinly sliced
3 large garlic cloves, finely chopped
125 ml (½ cup) dry white wine
300 g (10½ oz) Swiss brown mushrooms,
 sliced
2 teaspoons chopped fresh thyme
300 ml (10½ oz) thick (double/heavy) cream
2 smoked chicken breast fillets, thinly sliced
350 g (12 oz) fresh linguine

1 Heat the oil in a saucepan. Add the leek and cook, stirring, over low heat for 3–4 minutes, or until soft. Add the garlic and cook for another minute. Pour in the wine and simmer for 2–3 minutes, or until the liquid has reduced by half.

2 Increase the heat to medium, add the mushrooms and thyme and cook for 5 minutes, or until any excess liquid has been absorbed, then add the cream and sliced chicken. Reduce the heat and simmer for 4–5 minutes, or until the sauce has slightly thickened. Meanwhile, cook the pasta in a large saucepan of boiling water until al dente. Drain and divide among serving plates. Spoon on the sauce and serve.

Simmer together leek, garlic and wine until reduced by half.

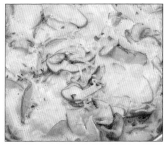

Add cream and sliced chicken and simmer until sauce has thickened.

Peppered Pork, Zucchini and Garganelli

PREPARATION TIME: 15 minutes
COOKING TIME: 25 minutes
SERVES 4

450 g (1 lb) pork fillet
3–4 teaspoons cracked black peppercorns
80 g (2¾ oz) butter
250 g (9 oz) garganelli
1 onion, halved and thinly sliced
2 large zucchini (courgettes), thinly sliced
20 g (⅔ cup) fresh basil, torn
155 g (¾ cup) baby black olives
60 g (½ cup) grated Romano cheese

1 Cut the pork fillet in half widthways and roll in the pepper and some salt. Heat half the butter in a large deep frying pan, add the pork and cook for 4 minutes each side, or until golden brown and just cooked through. Remove from the pan and cut into 5 mm (¼ inch) slices, then set aside and keep warm.

2 Cook the pasta in a large saucepan of boiling water until al dente; drain well and return to the pan. Meanwhile, melt the remaining butter in the frying pan, add the onion and cook, stirring, over medium heat for about 3 minutes, or until soft. Add the zucchini and toss for 5 minutes, or until starting to soften. Add the basil, olives, sliced pork and any juices and toss well. Stir the pork mixture through the hot pasta, then season to taste with salt and ground black pepper. Serve immediately, topped with the cheese.

Cook pork fillet until golden brown and cut into thin slices.

Add pork to other ingredients, add pasta and top with cheese.

Cotelli, Tomato and Artichoke Grill

PREPARATION TIME: 15 minutes
COOKING TIME: 20 minutes
SERVES 4

350 g (12 oz) cotelli
285 g (10 oz) jar marinated artichoke
  hearts, drained and chopped
2 tablespoons olive oil
250 ml (1 cup) thick (double/heavy) cream
2 tablespoons chopped fresh thyme
2 garlic cloves, crushed
75 g (¾ cup) grated Parmesan cheese
210 g (1⅔ cups) grated Cheddar cheese
950 g (2 lb 2 oz) tomatoes, cut into
  5 mm (¼ inch) slices

1 Cook the pasta in a large saucepan of boiling water until al dente. Drain; return to the pan. Grease a 23 cm x 30 cm (9 inch x 12 inch) rectangular ovenproof dish. Stir the artichokes, olive oil, cream, thyme, garlic, half the Parmesan and 155 g (1¼ cups) of the Cheddar through the pasta and season. Spread evenly in the dish.

2 Arrange the tomatoes over the top, overlapping one another. Season, then sprinkle with the remaining cheese. Cook under a hot grill (broiler) for 6 minutes, or until the cheeses melt and are golden brown.

Spread pasta and cheese mixture evenly through ovenproof dish.

Top with tomatoes, season, and sprinkle with remaining cheese.

Fresh Fettucine with Balsamic Seared Tuna Chunks

PREPARATION TIME: 15 minutes +
10 minutes marinating
COOKING TIME: 15 minutes
SERVES 4–6

4 x 200 g (7 oz) tuna steaks
170 ml (⅔ cup) balsamic vinegar
125 ml (½ cup) good-quality olive oil
1 lemon
1 garlic clove, finely chopped
1 red onion, finely chopped
2 tablespoons capers, rinsed and dried
10 g (½ cup) fresh flat-leaf (Italian) parsley,
  finely chopped
500 g (1 lb 2 oz) fresh fettucine

1 Place tuna in a non-metallic dish and cover with balsamic vinegar. Turn to coat evenly with vinegar and marinate for 10 minutes. Heat 2 tablespoons of the oil in a large frying pan over medium heat and cook tuna steaks for 2–3 minutes each side. Remove from the pan, cut into 2 cm (¾ inch) cubes and transfer to a bowl.

2 Finely grate rind from lemon to give ½ teaspoon zest, then squeeze the lemon to give 60 ml (¼ cup) juice. Wipe frying pan clean, and heat 2 tablespoons of olive oil over medium heat, then add garlic and cook for 30 seconds. Stir in chopped onion and cook for 2 minutes. Add lemon zest and capers and cook for 1 minute, then stir in parsley and cook for 1 minute. Add lemon juice and remaining oil and gently toss together. Season to taste.

3 Meanwhile, cook the pasta in a large saucepan of boiling water until al dente. Drain well, return to the pan and toss the caper mixture through. Divide the pasta among serving bowls and arrange the tuna pieces over the top.

Cut seared tuna into small cubes and place in a bowl.

Cook together garlic, onion, lemon zest, capers and parsley.

Stir caper and parsley mixture through pasta, and top with tuna.

Cresti di Gallo with Creamy Tomato and Bacon Sauce

PREPARATION TIME: 10 minutes

COOKING TIME: 15 minutes

SERVES 4

400 g (14 oz) cresti di gallo
1 tablespoon olive oil
170 g (6 oz) streaky bacon, thinly sliced
   500 g (1 lb 2 oz) Roma (plum) tomatoes,
   roughly chopped
125 ml (½ cup) thick (double/heavy) cream
2 tablespoons sun-dried (sun-blushed)
   tomato pesto
2 tablespoons finely chopped fresh flat-leaf
   (Italian) parsley
50 g (½ cup) finely grated Parmesan cheese

1 Cook the pasta in a large saucepan of boiling water until al dente. Drain and return to the pan. Meanwhile, heat the oil in a frying pan, add the bacon and cook over high heat for 2 minutes, or until starting to brown. Reduce the heat to medium, add the tomato and cook, stirring frequently, for 2 minutes, or until the tomato has softened but still holds its shape.

2 Stir in the cream and pesto until heated through. Remove from heat, add the parsley, then toss the sauce and Parmesan through the pasta.

Cook together the bacon and tomato, until tomato is soft.

Add cream, pesto and parsley, then toss sauce through pasta.

Orzo and Greek Cheese Bake

PREPARATION TIME: 15 minutes
COOKING TIME: 40 minutes
SERVES 6

415 g (2 cups) orzo
60 g (2¼ oz) butter
6 spring onions (scallions), chopped
450 g (1 lb) English spinach, stems removed,
  rinsed well and chopped
2 tablespoons plain (all-purpose) flour
1.25 litres (5 cups) milk
250 g (9 oz) kefalotyri cheese, grated
250 g (9 oz) marinated feta cheese, drained
3 tablespoons chopped fresh dill

1 Preheat the oven to 190°C (375°F/Gas 5). Cook the pasta in a large pan of boiling water until al dente. Drain well, then return to the pan. Heat 20 g (½ oz) butter in a large pan over high heat and cook the spring onion for 30 seconds. Add the spinach and stir for 1 minute, or until wilted. Season; stir into the orzo.

2 Put the remaining butter in the saucepan in which the spinach was cooked. Melt over low heat, then stir in the flour and cook for 1 minute, or until pale and foaming. Remove from the heat and gradually stir in the milk. Return to the heat and stir constantly for 5 minutes, or until the sauce boils and thickens. Add two thirds of the kefalotyri and all of the feta and stir for 2 minutes until melted and well mixed. Remove from the heat and stir in the dill.

3 Combine the pasta mix with the cheese sauce, season and pour into a greased 2.5 litre (10 cup) ovenproof ceramic dish. Sprinkle the remaining cheese on top. Bake for 15 minutes.

Stir together the wilted spinach and the cooked pasta.

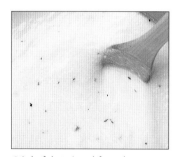
Stir kefalotyri and feta cheeses into milk mixture until melted.

Mix pasta into cheese sauce, pour into ovenproof dish, and bake.

Tagliatelle with Salmon and Creamy Dill Dressing

PREPARATION TIME: 10 minutes
COOKING TIME: 15 minutes
SERVES 4

350 g (12 oz) fresh tagliatelle
60 ml (¼ cup) olive oil
3 x 200 g (7 oz) salmon fillets, skinned and boned (ask your fishmonger to do this for you)
3 garlic cloves, crushed
375 ml (1½ cups) cream
1½ tablespoons chopped fresh dill
1 teaspoon mustard powder
1 tablespoon lemon juice
40 g (1½ oz) shaved Parmesan cheese

1 Cook the pasta in a large saucepan of boiling water until al dente. Drain, then toss with 1 tablespoon oil. Meanwhile, heat the remaining oil in a deep frying pan; cook the salmon for 2 minutes each side, or until crisp on the outside but still pink inside. Remove from the pan, cut into 2 cm (¾ inch) cubes; keep warm.

2 In the same pan, add the garlic and cook for 30 seconds, or until fragrant. Add the cream, dill and mustard powder, bring to the boil, then reduce the heat and simmer, stirring, for 4–5 minutes, or until thickened. Season.

3 Add the salmon and any juices plus the lemon juice to the dill sauce and stir until warm. Gently toss the salmon sauce through the pasta and divide among four serving bowls. Sprinkle with Parmesan and serve.

Cut cooked salmon into small cubes and keep warm.

Cook together garlic, cream, dill and mustard powder until thick.

Add salmon and lemon juice to dill sauce and stir until warm.

Fricelli with Mushrooms and Rocket

PREPARATION TIME: 15 minutes +
10 minutes soaking
COOKING TIME: 15 minutes
SERVES 4

10 g (¼ oz) dried porcini mushrooms
375 g (13 oz) fricelli
25 g (1 oz) butter
60 ml (¼ cup) extra virgin olive oil
2 garlic cloves, crushed
250 g (9 oz) button mushrooms, sliced
60 ml (¼ cup) lemon juice
35 g (⅓ cup) grated Parmesan cheese
80 g (2¾ oz) baby rocket (arugula) leaves,
  trimmed

1 Soak the porcini in 80 ml (⅓ cup) boiling water for 10 minutes, or until softened. Cook the pasta in a large saucepan of boiling water until al dente. Drain and return to the pan.

2 Meanwhile, heat the butter and oil over medium heat in a frying pan. Add the garlic and button mushrooms and cook for 4 minutes, tossing occasionally. Drain the porcini, reserving the soaking liquid. Chop all of the mushrooms, then add to the frying pan with the reserved soaking liquid. Bring to a simmer.

3 Add the mushroom mixture, lemon juice and Parmesan to the saucepan with the pasta and toss together. Season to taste with salt and ground black pepper. Toss through the rocket just before serving. Spoon into warm serving bowls and serve.

Soak porcini mushrooms in boiling water until softened.

Drain porcini, add to pan with soaking liquid and simmer.

Add mushroom mixture, lemon juice and Parmesan to pasta.

Spaghetti Primavera

PREPARATION TIME: 15 minutes
COOKING TIME: 15 minutes
SERVES 4

400 g (14 oz) spaghetti
80 ml (⅓ cup) extra virgin olive oil
200 g (7 oz) fresh asparagus, trimmed and
  cut into 5 cm (2 inch) lengths
155 g (1 cup) frozen peas
155 g (1 cup) frozen broad (fava) beans
1 leek, thinly sliced
2 tablespoons finely chopped fresh flat-leaf
  (Italian) parsley
250 ml (1 cup) thick (double/heavy) cream
35 g (⅓ cup) grated Parmesan cheese

1 Cook the pasta in a large saucepan of boiling water until al dente. Rinse and drain well, then return to the pan, toss with 2 tablespoons of the oil and keep warm.

2 Meanwhile, bring a saucepan of water to the boil and cook the asparagus and peas for 2 minutes, or until bright green and tender. Remove with a slotted spoon and plunge into cold water. Return the pan to the boil and cook the broad beans for 2 minutes, or until tender. Drain, cool, then slip off their skins.

3 Heat the remaining oil in a frying pan and cook the leek over low heat for 2–3 minutes, or until soft but not brown. Add the blanched vegetables and cook for 1 minute, or until warmed through. Stir in the parsley and cream and simmer for 2–3 minutes. Toss the sauce and Parmesan through the pasta, season well and serve.

Toss cooked and drained pasta with 2 tablespoons olive oil.

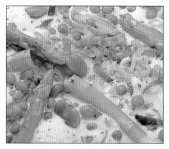

Cook asparagus and peas until bright green and tender.

Zucchini Pasta Bake

PREPARATION TIME: 15 minutes
COOKING TIME: 40 minutes
SERVES 4

200 g (7 oz) risoni
40 g (1½ oz) butter
4 spring onions (scallions), thinly sliced
400 g (14 oz) zucchini (courgettes), grated
4 eggs
125 ml (½ cup) cream
100 g (3½ oz) ricotta cheese
100 g (⅔ cup) grated mozzarella cheese
75 g (¾ cup) grated Parmesan cheese

1 Preheat the oven to 180°C (350°F/Gas 4). Cook the pasta in a large saucepan of boiling water until al dente. Drain well. Meanwhile, heat the butter in a frying pan, cook the spring onion for 1 minute, then add the zucchini and cook for a further 4 minutes, or until soft. Cool slightly.

2 Combine the eggs, cream, ricotta, mozzarella, risoni and half of the Parmesan well. Stir in the zucchini mixture. Season. Spoon into four 500 ml (2 cup) greased ovenproof dishes, but not to the brim. Sprinkle with the remaining Parmesan and cook for 25–30 minutes, or until firm and golden.

Combine eggs, cream, cheeses and risoni and add to zucchini mix.

Spoon into small overproof dishes and cook for 25–30 minutes.

Warm Lamb, Pasta and Chargrilled Capsicum Salad

PREPARATION TIME: 15 minutes +
10 minutes standing
COOKING TIME: 30 minutes
SERVES 6

125 ml (½ cup) olive oil
1 tablespoon chopped fresh rosemary
2 garlic cloves, crushed
400 g (14 oz) lamb fillets (backstrap)
60 g (¼ cup) wholegrain mustard
400 g (14 oz) fricelli
250 g (9 oz) snow peas (mangetout), trimmed
320 g (2 cups) ready-made chargrilled, skinned red capsicum (pepper), thinly sliced
100 g (3½ oz) Swiss cheese, shaved

1 Preheat oven to 190°C (375°F/Gas 5). Place oil, rosemary and garlic in a frying pan and cook, stirring, over low heat for 2 minutes. Strain oil into large bowl, then return half of it to the pan. Add rosemary and garlic to bowl. Reheat frying pan over high heat, add lamb; cook for 30 seconds each side, or until browned. Transfer lamb to a baking dish and roast for 8 minutes; rest for 10 minutes.

2 Pour any remaining oil from frying pan and any juices from baking dish into bowl with the rosemary and garlic. Add mustard and stir well. While meat rests, cook pasta in a large saucepan of boiling water. Drain and transfer to bowl with oil mixture. Bring a saucepan of water to the boil, add snow peas and cook for 30 seconds, then drain and set aside.

3 Thinly slice lamb on the diagonal and place in the bowl with pasta. Add snow peas, capsicum and two thirds of the cheese. Season with salt and pepper. Toss together. Divide among four serving plates or bowls and sprinkle with the remaining cheese.

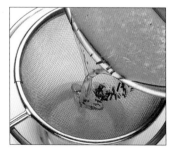

Cook together oil, rosemary and garlic, then strain into bowl.

Add mustard and roasting juices to bowl with oil mixture.

Slice lamb and place in the bowl with pasta and oil mixture.

Tagliatelle with Feta, Tomato and Rocket

PREPARATION TIME: 15 minutes
COOKING TIME: 15 minutes
SERVES 4

4 vine-ripened tomatoes
1 small red onion, finely chopped
4 tablespoons shredded fresh basil
2 tablespoons olive oil
375 g (13 oz) tagliatelle
2 garlic cloves, finely chopped
150 g (5½ oz) baby rocket (arugula) leaves
150 g (5½ oz) soft feta cheese, crumbled
15 g (¼ cup) fresh small whole basil leaves

1 Score a cross in the base of each tomato, then place in a bowl of boiling water for 1 minute. Plunge into cold water and peel the skin away from the cross. Cut in half and remove the seeds with a teaspoon. Chop, then transfer to a bowl. Add the onion and basil, stir in 1 tablespoon of the oil and set aside.

2 Cook the pasta in a large saucepan of boiling water until al dente. Drain, reserving 125 ml (½ cup) pasta water. Return the pasta to the pan, add the remaining oil, the garlic and reserved pasta water, tossing over medium heat for 1–2 minutes until warm. Stir in the tomato mixture, rocket and feta. Season. Divide among four plates and garnish with basil leaves.

Chop tomato, add onion and basil and 1 tablespoon and oil.

Toss cooked pasta over medium heat with garlic and oil.

All our recipes are thoroughly tested in a specially developed test kitchen. Standard metric measuring cups and spoons are used in the development of our recipes. All cup and spoon measurements are level. We have used 60 g (2¼ oz/Grade 3) eggs in all recipes. Sizes of cans vary from manufacturer to manufacturer and between countries – use the can size closest to the one suggested in the recipe.

CONVERSION GUIDE

1 cup = 250 ml (9 fl oz)

1 teaspoon = 5 ml

1 Australian tablespoon = 20 ml (4 teaspoons)

1 UK/US tablespoon = 15 ml (3 teaspoons)

Where temperature ranges are indicated, the lower figure applies to gas ovens, the higher to electric ovens. This allows for the fact that the flame in gas ovens generates a drier heat, which effectively cooks food faster than the moister heat of an electric oven, even if the temperature setting is the same.

DRY MEASURES	LIQUID MEASURES	LINEAR MEASURES
30 g = 1 oz	30 ml = 1 fl oz	6 mm = ¼ inch
250 g = 9 oz	125 ml = 4 fl oz	1 cm = ½ inch
500 g = 1 lb 2 oz	250 ml = 9 fl oz	2.5 cm = 1 inch

CUP CONVERSIONS – DRY INGREDIENTS

1 cup almonds, slivered whole = 125 g (4½ oz)

1 cup cheese, lightly packed processed cheddar = 155 g (5½ oz)

1 cup wheat flour = 125 g (4½ oz)

1 cup wholemeal flour = 140 g (5 oz)

1 cup minced (ground) meat = 250 g (9 oz)

1 cup pasta shapes = 125 g (4½ oz)

1 cup raisins = 170 g (6 oz)

1 cup rice, short grain, raw = 200 g (7 oz)

1 cup sesame seeds = 160 g (6 oz)

1 cup split peas = 250 g (9 oz)

	°C	°F	GAS MARK
Very slow	120	250	½
Slow	150	300	2
Mod slow	160	325	3
Moderate	180	350	4
Mod hot	190(g)–210(e)	375–425	5
Hot	200(g)–240(e)	400–475	6
Very hot	230(g)–260(e)	450–525	8

(g) = gas (e) = electric

Note: For fan-forced ovens, check your appliance manual, but as a general rule, set the oven temperature to 20°C lower than the temperature indicated in the recipe.

INTERNATIONAL GLOSSARY

capsicum	sweet bell pepper	cornflour	cornstarch
chick pea	garbanzo bean	eggplant	aubergine
chilli	chile, chili pepper	spring onion	scallion
		zucchini	courgette

First published in 2004 by Murdoch Books Pty Limited.

Erico House, 6th Floor North, 93-99 Upper Richmond Road, Putney, London, SW15 2TG, United Kingdom.

This edition published in 2007 for INDEX: Garrard Way, Kettering, NN16 8TD, United Kingdom.

ISBN-13: 978 1 921259 71 5   ISBN-10: 1 921259 71 X

Printed by Sing Cheong Printing Co. Ltd. PRINTED IN CHINA.